ACKNOWLEDGEMENTS

I'd like to thank all the people who have encouraged and supported me throughout the making of *Cut It Out!* Thank you to Elen for championing this book and coming up with such a wonderful working title. Thank you to Alice and Daisy at Found for cheering me on and making it possible.

Thank you to my WORK IT family and the girls at The W Project.
To all my tutors at The Royal Drawing School for teaching me
how to see.
To all my friends at Kingston University.
To every single one of my students, I adore you.

A special thank you to Clare, Swizz, Lakwena and all my friends for keeping me going. Especially my beautiful girls Tara and Safia for their love and sisterhood.

Jonny, what would I do without you? Thank you again and again,
I love you.

Thank you to my wonderful family and to my darling dad, Jock the Scot.
And to my heroes Anna and Redha, I am eternally grateful.

2

Virgin Books, an imprint of Ebury Publishing,
20 Vauxhall Bridge Road,
London SW1V 2SA

Virgin Books is part of the Penguin Random House group of companies whose addresses can be found at global.penguinrandomhouse.com

Penguin
Random House
UK

MIX
Paper from
responsible sources
FSC® C018179

Penguin Random House is committed to a sustainable future for our business, our readers and our planet.
This book is made from Forest Stewardship Council® certified paper.

The activities in this book require the use of a scalpel and should be performed with great care and under adult supervision. Neither the author nor publishers can accept responsibility for any loss, damage or injuries that may occur as a result of these activities, and the author and publishers disclaim as far as the law allows any liability arising directly or indirectly from the use, or misuse, of the information contained in this book.

CUT IT OUT!

30 DESIGNS TO CUT OUT AND KEEP

POPPY CHANCELLOR

Virgin BOOKS

FOR MY LITTLE SISTER IRIS
AND THE NEXT GENERATION
OF TINY WOMEN LEGENDS

INTRODUCTION

Cut It Out! is a totally new approach to the art of papercutting, which will inspire you and give you confidence to unleash that sparkling self-expression that we all have locked away in our creativity closet. These unique designs will teach you a whole new craft and instill in you the belief that you can create your own designs, too. I believe that we all need time to be artistic, whatever your day-to-day profession. It's good for your brain and soul whichever way you look at it.

In this book you will learn all the techniques you will need, be treated to lots of tips and be given loads of templates to get you started with your new hobby. The 30 templates in these pages will help you to cut out and personalise your own gifts, presents and artworks. Everything you might need for a special occasion has been thought of, and you'll soon have the reputation amongst friends and family for being savvy with a scalpel – in a good way! However, I must warn you that once you get started you're sure to get lots of requests to create bespoke and beautiful pieces for all your friends.

I'll also teach you how to frame, cut and design your own papercuts with all the must-know expert tips you need to be a cut above the rest. The process is simple and the outcome is thrilling. You don't need much skill to be able to cut along a suggested line, but practice and patience is essential. Anyone with a scalpel and a steady hand is encouraged to give this a try; I guarantee you will be impressed by your own efforts and mesmerised by the results.

There is something very soothing in this art of taking your time. When you patiently follow the lines with the knife, you will start to see elegant artistry emerge from a single sheet of paper. The hours slip away and all those daily naggings about 'why do I look pregnant after eating pasta?' and 'will I ever be able to walk in heels?' start to dim. Your mind becomes utterly focused on the task in hand. Creating wonderful images out of a single piece of paper is beyond satisfying, even for a novice. Before long, you too will understand the pleasure of people asking: 'How did you do that?!'

I had never considered papercutting as anything other than an octogenarian hobby until a few years ago, when it experienced a glorious resurgence. As a child I remember being fascinated by book illustrations created in silhouette and shadow plays, but it all seemed so different to the art I would see celebrated in London's galleries. I wanted to create something that was my own.

Throughout my time at art school I tried my hand at everything, but nothing quite seemed to fit. I enjoyed drawing; I endlessly sketched my dogs sleeping, my mum sleeping, a woman on the tube sleeping … I see my papercuts as a type of 3D drawing, as little sculptures in their own right. I enjoy the thrill of seeing my sketches come to life in the physical world. I remember the moment when I began to cut out people's profiles on the bus, inspired by Victorian silhouettes. The directness and the restriction of having to cut something out intrigued me. I loved that the paper could tear or break as I worked with it, and the fragility of the designs became something that fascinated me.

After a few late nights obsessing over my cutting mat, I started to feel comfortable and encouraged. I started making everything from paper – bunting, cards and even large installations. I was on hand with a scalpel or scissors to add an embellishment wherever it was needed. The demand for something hand-made and accessible is fast becoming priceless in a commercial world of the mass-produced. I am always proud to say, 'I did that.'

I've always had a short attention span and zero patience so papercutting didn't come naturally to me. Now it seems to kick in almost instantly – every time I pick up a scalpel. When I look back at those days when I was teaching myself this art form, I'm always quite amazed. I have created a career out of something I loved and learned on my own and now, five years later, I'm

working with brands I admire, creating events and artworks that are such a pleasure to be part of. I have my own studio and a network of creatives who encourage me and inspire me to keep going.

The 'do-it-yourself' revolution of crafting has thrown a whole array of arts and techniques into the spotlight, and papercutting deserves to have its moment, too. As we become more self- and phone-obsessed, spending time making things seems to be an oasis in our hectic schedules. The complexity of these designs doesn't make them impossible, it just means you can schedule a little more me-time into your day to get them done. Relax, and take some time out to make something amazing.

If you don't have a physical creative network to rely on, social media can be a really helpful way to share ideas and find inspiration. Start following paper artists and other creatives who feed your mind. Share your own creations online and show off your new skills. Getting feedback is lovely, especially if you're a bit of an introvert who works modestly at home. Praise is nourishing for everybody. I'd like to encourage you to use this book as a guiding light for how to do it your way.

Whether you keep your papercuts, use them for an occasion, frame them or give them away, these designs have a sense of humour and character that will keep you occupied from start to finish. This book is divided into different occasions with accompanying designs to show you how to use a template for a multitude of different events. Keep this book as something you pull out when you need a gift for a friend or when you just feel like relaxing and making something for yourself.

Don't feel you have to stick to the chapters rigidly; some things may work for other scenarios and you can adapt them with your new papercutting skills. Birthday cards, Halloween decorations and party masks are all part of your papercutting kit, so let's see what we need in order to get started.

MATERIALS

There are thousands of ways to transform a piece of paper. You can tear, colour, fold and destroy it, and there are also many different ways by which you can do these things. It's the same when you're making a papercut – there are a load of options. I'm going to tell you what I use and what you could use, but I encourage you to get a bit Edward Scissorhands on the whole thing – experiment and find your own niche.

The basic tools that you need, though, are: a cutting mat, scalpel and some paper. The great thing about papercutting is that you don't need very much to get started, and it won't cost you the world.

SUPPLIES

My favourite stationery stockists are:
London Graphic Centre, *londongraphics.co.uk*
Atlantis Art Materials, *atlantisart.co.uk*
Cowling & Wilcox, *cowlingandwilcox.com*
Shepherds inc. Falkiner Fine Papers, *store.bookbinding.co.uk*

These are my two favourite shops to visit:
Choosing Keeping on Columbia Road in London,
    choosingkeeping.com
L. Cornelissen and Son near London's British Museum,
    cornelissen.com

And here some other websites I recommend:
Fiskars.co.uk (scalpels)
Xacto.com (scalpels)
Maderia.co.uk (scissors)
Gfsmith.com (paper)
Fedrigoni.com (paper)
Nkuku.com (picture frames)

You can also search online to find your local suppliers.

CUTTING MAT

Firstly, you'll need a self-healing cutting mat (they come in hot pink, too…). I'd suggest getting anything bigger than A4 size to comfortably cover your workspace – mine is A2.

SCALPEL

Next you'll need a scalpel. You can buy scalpels in most art shops and a regular craft scalpel will work well with these designs. I would advise against the chunkier craft knives used for cutting tougher materials like card or wood, though. I use a pointed surgical scalpel by Swann-Morton with a number 3 handle and 10A blades (available at well-stocked art shops or online). Make sure you have a healthy supply of blades, as these will need to be changed regularly.

If you suffer from arthritis or you would prefer something a bit more comfortable, there are options like the Fiskars fingertip knife, which has a finger setting designed to reduce pressure on it. Also there are some amazing padded knives and scalpels that add comfort to your grip, like the designers' range from X-Acto.

You can also look into using a swivel blade if you're having difficulties cutting curved lines, but I would suggest you experiment and see what suits you.

A very serious note about sharp objects. Obviously we are using scalpels throughout this book and I'm keen for you to respect your tools and stay safe! Please take the utmost care when using your scalpel and children will need to be supervised.

SCISSORS AND HOLE PUNCHES

Some people use scissors to make their papercuts. Although I prefer to use a scalpel, I do find it useful to have a pair of small scissors to hand to help trim edges or cut away larger borders. Madeira have a great selection to choose from and I've always loved their golden stork scissors.

You might also like to keep a single hole punch handy for cutting out small circles as ribbon loops for masks or baubles.

PAPER

In this book we will provide the paper and templates for you to work from, but if you'd like to keep the book intact you could trace the designs onto other colours or weights of paper. I would suggest any paper between 150–170gsm; card is tougher to get through with your scalpel and origami paper may be too thin. I'm a huge fan of colour and you can get some beautiful paper from stockists such as G.F. Smith and Fedrigoni. My personal fave is jet-black Canford paper by Daler-Rowney. I love using black just as much as a bold colour.

PRESENTING YOUR PAPERCUT

When you have completed your papercut, there are endless ways to use and display your finished piece. Here are a few fun suggestions that will work with all the templates in this book.

PARTIES AND BIRTHDAYS
Transform your papercuts into gift cards by mounting them onto brightly coloured card. You can slot your designs together to create freestanding table settings, or personalise and frame them for the ultimate thoughtful birthday present. Don't be shy to wear your party mask design, just loop ribbon through the holes.

LOVE FEST
Show someone you care with these heart-warming designs. You can mount them on bright coloured card and send them out as saucy greetings. Frame them and deliver your lover a handmade gift, or use gold photo corners to add a touch of glamour to your cute cut-out. Whichever way you present your papercut, you'll be sure to have a queue of admirers wanting more.

WEDDINGS
Make sure you exploit your wedding designs to the full! They can be used for cake decorations, have ribbon or string threaded through them for bunting or even added into the flower display. You can also make the perfect paper anniversary gift or bridal thank-you cards. I love providing a touch of glamour by adding details with metallic pens or liquid gold ink.

ANIMALS
These animal designs are amazingly versatile and can be used pretty much anywhere, for anything! You can add them to your pinboard, tack them onto the windows and even decorate your favourite notebook or diary with them. They look wonderful in children's bedrooms, especially tucked underneath a lampshade.

HALLOWEEN
Get creative with your papercuts by stringing them up into decorations, hanging them on the front door or even incorporate them into your costume as a brooch or hair accessory – who knows? Have fun trying out a few different possibilities.

CHRISTMAS
These designs are perfect for every aspect of a beautiful Christmas. Send out your papercuts in the post as baubles or Christmas cards by mounting them and attaching ribbon. Hang them on your own tree or use them as table settings (just not too near candles!). Use the concertina designs as decorations around the house, as cards or as the centrepiece of your Christmas dinner.

HOW TO FRAME AND DISPLAY YOUR PAPERCUTS

I'm going to give you options from cheap to chic and you can choose which one complements your paper occasion. You can mount your papercut onto coloured card or frame them yourself.

Photo corners act as a great basic mount because they're non-permanent. Unlike glue, photo corners are ideal to use because they allow your papercut to be detached from the mount, which gives you the option of framing it at a later date. They come in gold, silver, black and also translucent, which is a very subtle option.

Sticky foam pads are another great way of creating a floating mount. Don't stick them down with PVA glue, though, because if you glue paper cuts to a mount they can wrinkle and look flat. Using pads allows the papercut to appear as if it's hovering off the board, creating a beautiful shadow. Some of your designs may be too intricate in some areas to stick on the pad, so either stick the pad to the slightly thicker areas of paper or cut them down to your preferred size.

I love **frames** that highlight the intricacy of the papercut. Frames with two panes of glass and no mount are perfect for this. Nkuku have some wonderful glass frames that allow you to add in artworks that appear to float. All you need is a few small pieces of double-sided tape attached to the back to make sure the artwork stays firmly in place and doesn't slip. Habitat have a similar frame called a 'Bacall' which does the job well.

If you're getting something framed especially, make sure you discuss the possibility of having a floating mount with your framer. Also, please make it very clear which way round the artwork needs to face, as papercuts can look very similar on either side and you don't want it permanently framed back to front! Learn from my mistakes …

It is also worth having a think about the colour of your frame and mount – do you go for something subtle and complementary, or clashing and contemporary? Depending on the occasion, subject of the piece or just whatever mood you're in, the frame and mount can really transform your papercut. Go with what you love and you can't go wrong.

Scanning allows you to replicate your papercut and send it to others. If you're handy with a computer and editing applications you can scan in your papercut and email it to people with accompanying text. For the more traditional among us, you can simply create a double-sided photocopy with the papercut on one side and your text on the other. This could work for party invites or thank-yous.

PRACTICE SHEETS

Now it's time to have a stab at papercutting and cut some corners. Remember, this is about practising, getting acquainted with your scalpel and trying out a few techniques. Don't be afraid to fail and have a few slip-ups (but watch those fingers!); this is totally normal and something that still happens to the best of us!

The first thing to do is have your workspace ready (tea and biscuits are a must). Set your template or blank sheet of paper onto your cutting mat in front of you, make sure your scalpel is sharp and you're ready to go. I always put on some music and have a bit of a sing along to really help my concentration.

Hold your scalpel as you would a pencil and practise a few straight lines on a spare piece of paper. This allows you to gauge the sharpness of your blade. If you're not cutting a clean line, press a little harder and make sure your blade is not fully vertical but resting into your hand on a diagonal.

Straight lines are a great place to start for a beginner, so jump in with cutting some of the stars and jagged lines in the worksheet.

How to use the templates in this book:

- Shaded areas indicate the spaces that should be cut out.
- The grey line shows the outline.
- Where you see dotted lines around text, these are optional so you can swap in your own words and phrases.
- Fold along the dashes on the concertinas.
- And if you want to remove the pages, there's a handy guideline near the gutter.

TIPS

Here are a few basic tips to remember when you start papercutting:

A sharp blade

A blunt blade is very likely to tear your paper; sharp blades allow for cleaner cuts. Make sure you change your blade every 2–3 hours. You can safely remove your blade with pliers, or most craft knives simply swivel open to release.

Cut back to front

All of the images you'll work from in this book are designed back to front. This means you'll be cutting the back of the design and when you're finished you can flip it over, leaving a clean finish with no guidelines or pencil marks visible from your initial design.

Always cut towards yourself

You'll have more control by cutting towards you. Remember to keep turning the paper round as you cut the design. It's also good to use your other hand to keep the paper flat and in place so that it doesn't wrinkle while you're cutting.

Cut the details first

By cutting the smallest sections first you'll be less likely to tear the intricate parts. Work up to the larger sections and outline so that the strength of the paper can support your design. If some parts of a design seem too intricate for you, just leave them out! You can also use specialised hole punches or pins to create the smaller circles in your design.

Let your lines overlap

When two lines that you're cutting meet, make sure the lines meet fully, otherwise you're left with a section of paper, which creates a bit of fluff when torn out of the design. You can prevent this by slightly overcutting the line. This gives your work a clean, professional finish, and seeing as we're cutting back to front, the overcut marks will be less visible on the other side.

Press nice and hard!

Work slowly and press hard. The harder you press the cleaner your cut will be (this also helps if you have a sharp blade). If you try to rush your papercutting, chances are the paper won't cut right through and it may tear.

CUTTING TIGHT CURVES AND CORNERS

Getting a clean curve can be difficult, especially when it's more acute. Swivel blades can be useful here as they move independently of the handle and allow you more fluidity. If you're tackling a curve with a regular scalpel, remember some of my previous tips:

- Don't cut it all in one go; try cutting one half of the curve and then the other.
- Cut towards you.

You can practise this on the semi-circles and flower designs in the worksheet.

When you're feeling more confident, move on to the bow and diamond design. Here you'll see you have to cut out the internal details first – the inside sections of the bow and diamond. It's all practice, so don't be too precious about your work just yet.

CUTTING CIRCLES

Circles are famously hard to cut, but personally, I'm a fan of the wonky circle – I love a bit of wonky imperfection and embrace it! That's the point of using our hands; we're not robots and we're prone to aesthetic imperfections. I love the charm of the handmade and the idea that a person actually took their time to make something.

When cutting a circle I like to divide up the work and take it a bit at a time. I cut a cross through the centre of the circle then cut round the edge a quarter at a time. This automatically stops us trying to cut the whole thing in one go (which can get a bit messy). You could also try rotating the paper as the scalpel cuts through it. Have a go at the section of large circles in the worksheet and then move on to the smaller centres of the flower designs.

If you like a more precise look, single-handed hole punches and other die cutters are great for creating uniform repeated shapes and patterns, so these might be a good way for you to get started with your own designs.

MIRRORED ALPHABET AND NUMBERS

Including text in your designs makes your finished papercut wonderfully personal. All at once it becomes a bespoke piece of art complete with your signature stamp. Whether it's a gift or something personal to keep, I love adding something unique.

Here's where the maths comes in … Seeing as all of our designs are back-to-front, we also need our text or digits to be back-to-front. I can never remember what a reverse 'G' or 'Z' looks like, so to save us the hassle I've drawn out an alphabet and some numbers here to help you.

Capital letters are always easier to cut out because they are made up of lovely bold and simple shapes. Some lower-case letters are harder, so it may help to draw the word you want to cut onto tracing paper the correct way round first, then flip it over to see what it will look like. If you're really stuck you can always use a mirror to double check if your letters will read correctly.

The key to adding in text is to make sure the letters are attached to the rest of the design. In these templates I've added scrolls, gaps or speech bubbles where you can add your chosen text. Remember, the letters must touch the edges of those designs or they'll simply fall out; ideally they should be attached in a minimum of two places to keep them firmly in the design, or attached to an adjoining letter. Make sure that what you write is clear and easy to read, don't cram too much in.

A B C D E F

G H I J K L

M N O P Q R

S T U V

W X Y

abcdefghi
jklmnopqr
stuvwxyz
0123456789
!"#$@&*

CREATING YOUR OWN DESIGNS

If you'd like to have a go at designing your own papercuts, here are a few things to remember:

1 /

You don't have to be good at drawing. You can always experiment with graphic patterns or geometric designs. This is a nice place to start if you have trouble drawing more figurative shapes.

2 /

Be clear about the positive and negative parts of your design; which parts will be solid paper and which bits will be cut out? I always put a little 'x' in the parts that will be cut away so I can work out the design visually.

3 /

Choose recognisable motifs. If you're drawing a silhouette of an object or creature, make sure it's clear. Simplify the shape and don't make it too complex. Ask yourself, 'Does this communicate the shape clearly?'

4 /

Make sure every element is connected to something else within the design. Don't get to the end of cutting and then realise your whole design is falling apart. Everything should be attached, like a fine lace. Use lines, decorative details and text to utilise areas of blank space.

5 /

This whole process is about experimentation; becoming a designer takes time. Use what you learn in this book to expand and encourage your own ideas and keep practising until it becomes a familiar graphic language that you can use with ease.

I've armed you with more than enough to get going. So it's time to get the bug and get started with your first papercut!

Poppy X

CHAPTER 1
PARTIES & BIRTHDAYS

In this chapter you'll find ideas for personalised cards, decorations, invites and accessories. Making something from this chapter is essential because turning up to a party empty-handed is the worst. It's almost as bad as turning up with a crap present you bought from the newsagent on the way there …

Luckily, help is at hand! Now that you're embarking on this new paper extravaganza you'll always be able to take time out to make something really special. Whether it's to decorate your own party or someone else's, these designs stand out.

PERSONALISED CARD
Add a birth date or some initials to keep the design simple and personal. Don't forget to use your mirrored alphabet as a reference.

HIGH-5IVES

These make beautiful cards.
Mount with foam pads onto
coloured card when you've
completed cutting.

PINEAPPLE CENTREPIECE

For this design you may want to copy the template onto some card or trace it onto slightly thicker paper. The two designs slot into each other to create a tropical, freestanding papercut.

PARTY INVITE

Get your jive shoes on and invite everyone round to your place for a knees-up! This papercut can be scanned as an e-vite or you can even photocopy your finished piece and add the details onto the reverse.

GATSBY MASK

Loop ribbon through each end of this design to wear as you please. Attach with double-sided tape or simply tie a knot in it to fasten.

CHAPTER 2
LOVE FEST

As a hopeless romantic,
Valentine's Day has always been a
bit of an event for me. Whether it's a heart-
smashing piñata party or an awkward date to the chip
shop, everyone's talking about it. You can make a papercut for
your lover, just for your fine self or even for someone you despise then burn
it into a thousand pieces! (It's very therapeutic.)

Let's be fair, when you give someone a papercut that took you hours to make, it's a pretty
obvious way of saying 'I like you' without even having to utter the words … Perfect!

With regards to the hen-do's, crafting is always a great way to get to know each other before
the strippers arrive. See if your gang can make some additional accessories for the bride's
wedding or just to make her feel unstoppable on her last night of disco-dancing freedom.

Here are a few designs to make you blush.

PIN ME UP

You can add a quote, phrase or even party details to this design, keeping it flirty and fun. Translucent photocorners could hold this little madam in place perfectly.

LOVERS' HEART

I've designed this romantic piece with two scrolls and a lovely rolling ampersand to allow you to add your desired names. A last name, nickname or pet name would do the job nicely!

BOTTOMS UP!

This cheeky design will bring smiles to men and women alike, making it the perfect gift. Add in your own word or name as the finishing touch.

KING AND QUEEN OF HEARTS

This piece is lovely as a romantic gift. Add in your own names to make it extra special. Remember to start with those little bits of detail first when you're cutting.

YOU AMPERSAND ME

This simple design won't take you too long to cut out. Practise adding in capital letters or numbers to make it truly personal.

CHAPTER 3
WEDDINGS

Rest assured that when you see someone showing off her massive diamond sparkler at the engagement party, she's really thinking of ways to save money, seeing as the whole budget's just been blown to smithereens.

WE'RE HERE TO HELP!, I hear you cry. Whether you're the maid of honour, father of the bride or the queen herself, get involved. Save a bit of cash by making these wonderful decorations and favours. Keep the wedding budget for the dancing horses and flamingos and cut a few corners with a cheeky bit of craft.

FLAGS OF LOVE

All you'll need is some thin wooden sticks or straws to attach the design to. Once you've taped the papercut to the stem you can use it as a cake topper or stick it into a bunch of flowers to add some Mexican-inspired flavour to your festivities.

FESTIVE BUNTING

Use the design as the template to cut through more than one sheet at a time. Using thin paper you can probably get about three triangles cut at once. Use your one-handed hole punch in both of the top corners and thread through ribbon or string.

HAND-HELD HEART
THANK-YOUS

Take some time out and get lost in this intricate hand-held heart design. Mount with sticky foam pads or scan it to send to everyone who attended.

PROTECTIVE HAND OF FATIMA

This is one of our stand-out designs and will take you slightly longer ecause of all that lovely detail. Once you've got confident with cutting, this is a triumph to complete.

PAPER ANNIVERSARY

A one-year anniversary is conveniently (for us) called a 'paper' anniversary, so we've just got to make them something!

We all love animals; they're cute and soft and less hassle than most of our friends. I've always loved drawing animals at the zoo or intensely studying my pet's facial expressions. So when I saw a Chinese papercut calendar full of different zodiac signs I was hooked. We'll look at some realistic and decorative designs to lead you into the papercutting wilderness populated by woodland and jungle creatures alike.

Allergic to cats? Make one instead!

BILKO THE CAT

This is a pretty intricate design, so make sure you're steady with your lines and take your time. Remember, if you ever slip up there's no harm in using a bit of sellotape on the back to reattach it.

BIRD DECORATIONS

These designs are ideal to have around your home. I love hanging them in windows or on plants. There is a loop added to some of the designs for hanging, but if you want to remove it, please do.

DECO RABBIT

Perfect for Easter, this bunny is a great element to add to any handmade occasion. You could use these as place settings or add a loop and just hang one on the front door to invite people in.

PARTY FOX

I love this mischievous fox. This is another design that works well in a window or bedroom. Make sure that you cut out the smaller interior details before you cut out the larger shapes and outline.

LOVELY LEOPARD

This leopard face is very intricate due to all the dots holding the design together. Remember you can leave out any bits that feel too intricate or difficult for you to cut. It will just be a slightly more simplified version, but no one will ever know!

It's time to terrify the neighbours and get crafty. Halloween is when you can go totally crazy with your creativity, paint your face, make an outfit and steal the show. Get ready for Halloween by adding some of these spooky essentials to your pound-shop hoard. If you're having a party these designs will add a bit of life to your day of the dead; they have a hint of Mexican heat, celebrating the morbid and macabre with dazzling patterns and motifs.

WELCOME SKELETON

Hang this guy on the fridge or on the door instead of the usual 'Keep out' signs. Use black ribbon or something more sinister to attach him to the desired resting place.

BAT BUNTING

This simple design can be cut out with scissors and then strung up for the desired spooky effect. Use red threads or sparkling black ribbons to add it to a shuddersome colour scheme. Remember you can always cut more than one bat at once by using the template over layers of paper.

SKULL SHOWSTOPPER

Take your time and enjoy the design gradually revealing itself as you cut away. Beautifully symbolic and highly decorative, this skull shows how you can bring a sense of humour and beauty to Halloween.

CREEPY CONCERTINA
This stand-up zig-zag fold design provide some deadly detail to your spooky set-up.

DEVILISH DARLING

Add some hot sauce to your Halloween with this welcome witch. Blu-tack to the window or under a lampshade for some saucy shadow play.

The best way to enjoy your family's company at Christmas time and keep everyone happy is to give them something fun and festive to do. I love enforcing my seasonal sweatshop of cousins, nieces and aunts to pitch in for the decoration collaboration.

It's fun to display papercuts in a range of different w ays throughout Christmas, especially as shadow play and lights. Lanterns, candles or fairy lights will create wonderful shadows for your artwork. I have tucked some of my designs inside lanterns, illuminated concertina designs with tea lights and even hung them from candlesticks.

Stringing up designs as wreaths or using them as table settings or cards adds a wonderful sense of occasion to your Christmas. Here are some great designs to hang from the rafters.

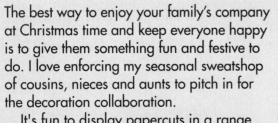

CRIMBO CONCERTINA

This Christmas landscape can be folded to become freestanding. Use this papercut as a decoration on the table or on your mantelpiece. You can rest tea lights behind it to create a delicate backlit effect.

STAR OF WONDER

This design slots into itself as a hanging decoration. You're welcome to glue it to join it together, but it also works without glue and folds flat easily when not stuck into place. String it up with ribbon or give it as a card or gift.

PAPER BAUBLES

Cut out these baubles for a wonderfully handmade Christmas. Attach them to the tree with ribbons and bows – alongside the tinsel and flamingos, obviously.

FOLD-OUT DUCK

This fold-out design will take you half the time. Fold the design down the middle to cut both sides at once. As you'll be cutting through two sheets of paper you'll need to press a little harder to make sure you're cutting right through. Then open up and you'll have a perfectly symmetrical design.

SNOWFLAKE

We've all had a go at making a paper snowflake in the past. Now it's time to upgrade a few levels to this delicate design and really show off.